Living in the Shadows:
Finding Strength
and Hope in Times
of Illness

Caring Companions
from Abbey Press

Living in the Shadows: Finding Strength and Hope in Times of Illness

Edited by Silas Henderson

ONE
CARING
PLACE

Abbey Press
St. Meinrad, IN 47577

Scripture quotes used by permission
from the New Revised Standard Version Bible,
copyrighted 1989.

Text © 2014 Abbey Press
Published by Abbey Press Publications
St. Meinrad, Indiana 47577
www.abbeypresspublications.com

Library of Congress Control Number
2014901703

ISBN 978-0-87029-655-0

Printed in the United States of America.

Introduction

❧

An old Sanskrit proverb, which is quoted by Daniel R. Grossoehme in his chapter "Facing Chronic Illness with Faith and Hope," reminds us that "today, well-lived / makes every yesterday a dream of happiness / and every tomorrow a vision of hope." Often, however, when we are living with illness, our worlds can become very small and seem to be little more than a steady procession of doctors visits, medical procedures, and tests, all within a cloud of pain, fatigue, and isolation.

Although none of us really has an answer as to "why" some of us must face the challenge of illness, we do have the power to ask a different question: "How can I face this illness with strength and hope?" In this small book, we have assembled a collection of *CareNotes* that best seem to address this second, better question head on.

It is our hope that this book will, indeed, be a source of strength, hope, and, above all, grace for you as you face the challenges that are unique to you and your specific illness. As you live in the shadow of today, may your tomorrow be filled with the light of the promise of health and wholeness.

—Silas Henderson

Contents

∾

Chapter I

Facing Chronic Illness With Faith and Hope

∾

By Daniel R. Grossoehme

Every day as I walk through the hospital where I work, I meet people living with chronic illness. And while no one I've met would have wished for their illness, many express gratitude for having learned what is really important in their lives. Their condition has helped them focus and decide where their priorities are in life. Spending time with the people they love takes on a new level of meaning.

Working your way through | A chronic illness is a condition that lasts longer than a year, places limits on what you are able to do, and requires medical or psychiatric care. Some chronic illnesses are rarely life-threatening; others are more serious.

Chronic illness may affect our bodies, or they may be chronic mental-health conditions such as depression or schizophrenia. The good news is, more than at any other time in the past, people today are able to live with a range of chronic illnesses (and sometimes more than one illness) due to advances in medications, physical therapy, and support.

❧ *Let yourself have a chronic illness gracefully.* As we move through the course of our lives, we change. None of us is the same person we were 10 years ago. Many events in our own lives, and in the lives of others around us, have altered us. Some of those changes are on the inside (how we see ourselves), and some of them may be on the outside, due to things that have happened to our bodies.

Living with a chronic illness changes people. People I have known who work on being whole while living with a chronic illness have some sense of their new identity. A middle-aged woman with ALS (Lou Gehrig's disease) told me that she felt as if she were a partially finished stone sculpture. She could feel the hammer blows, but because she was the sculpture, she couldn't see the emerging beauty only the Sculptor saw. Having that image helped her understand the place of pain in her life and her purpose in life, and gave her hope for her future.

Finding a metaphor to describe life can be healing because it gives meaning to our experiences. Having meaningful lives is one reason we have for going on in spite of adversity, even when going on can be a struggle. What is life like for you? Where do you find meaning?

∾ *Find a spiritual friend.* Look for someone who can share part of your journey through the experience of illness. This could be a pastoral minister, professional counselor, or a loved one who is well-grounded in their faith. The important thing is that the person be someone with whom you are comfortable sharing your questions, fears, and joys, and someone who will be available when you need support and companionship.

Yesterday is but a dream,
And tomorrow is only a vision.
But today, well-lived, makes every yesterday a dream of happiness,
And every tomorrow a vision of hope.
Look well, therefore, to this day.
—Sanskrit proverb

Years ago, offering spiritual support to someone with a chronic illness meant helping them grieve, period—focusing on the loss of who they had been and the life they would no longer lead. Now the focus is more on dealing with the person as they are, and helping them focus on that part of their identity that never changes—their status as one of God's beloved children.

Even though you may have a chronic illness, it doesn't "have" you. You are more than your illness. Focus on the "more."

❧ *Focus your energies on how to live with a chronic illness.* The unanswerable "why" questions are natural, human questions to ask. However, to focus only on "why" questions is to spiral into hopelessness.

Try to reframe your questions, asking instead, "Now that I have this disease, how am I going to live in faith and hope?" Although you may not be ready to answer the question until you have lived with the illness for some time, explore whether there are opportunities that are now open to you that might not have been without the chronic illness. Perhaps you can teach others about chronic conditions and the needs of

4

people who have them. Perhaps you can now focus on the people in your life in a new way, or maybe you can learn to set aside the daily rush and discover that there is joy in solitude.

❧ *Make time for yourself, and for God.* The very term chronic (from *chronos,* meaning *time*) makes it clear that this disease is all about time. And we don't just have time, we have "time for" something (time for going out with friends, time for going to the doctor, time for a haircut). Learning to make "time for" is an important step in seeking wholeness, even when a cure may not be possible.

Make time for others—and make time for yourself, too. Sometimes you may feel overwhelmed, that you simply can't make it all work out. Figure out what your priorities are. Decide early in the day what is most important for that one day, and don't try to do more than that. In this way you keep control of your life, rather than having the condition control it for you. Make an appointment with yourself for a particular day and time, and set aside a length of time for yourself ("Tonight after the kids are in bed, I'm going to soak in a bath for 20 minutes").

Time for God is also important. This doesn't have to be a formal prayer time, although it may be. Simply "wasting time with God" can be healing—consciously being aware of being in God's presence while you are doing something you enjoy or that is relaxing.

Try walking around a garden or a park, chatting with God silently in a rocking chair, or writing in a journal. Some people find it helpful to have a particular sacred space in their home or yard, perhaps with a few objects, such as a candle or a flower, that remind them of their humanity and of the holy. This space is set aside—being with God may be the only thing they do there. Wherever this space is, being there immediately brings them into conscious togetherness with what is divine in their lives.

One of the tragedies of lives broken by chronic illness is the isolation and loneliness that is often part of the experience. Separation from God makes that feeling worse. When and where do you feel especially connected to the holy, and how can you make time for this?

Circle me, O God,
Keep fear and disillusion
*   without.*
Bring a glimmer of hope
*   within.*
Circle me, O God,
Keep nightmare without.
Bring moments of rest
*   within.*
Circle me, O God,
Keep bitterness without.
Bring an occasional sense
Of your presence within.
      —Lyn Whittall and
           Judy Hager,
      Spirit of Gentleness:
      A Collection of Prayers
           and Meditations

❧ Focus your questions in a positive direction. One of my favorite questions in the hospital is, "What would make things turn out alright?" It's a question about hope, and about where new life is to be found. Hope is different from a wish, because hope implies a relationship (instead of a "thing" we wish for). We don't have to go through this alone. In experiencing the love and acceptance of others, we glimpse in a small way the divine love for each of us. Love will not cure us, but love makes us whole.

Another favorite question is, "So how are you and God doing?" Sometimes people seem embarrassed to admit that the answer isn't "Just fine!" but any relationship that is real will have its ups and downs. Living a faithful life means living one that is open and honest—and that includes acknowledging to yourself the normal ups and downs you experience in your faith life.

God is intensely interested in what humans are going through. Tell God what you are going through, and remind yourself that what you are experiencing is a perfectly normal part of any relationship. Sometimes, having "the way things are" cease to nourish us spiritually is a sign that we have grown and developed to a new level, and that the old ways of relating won't work any more. Although leaving old familiar ways behind can be a source of anxiety, it is also a sign of development on our part. It brings the promise of a new and deeper way of being related to what is ultimate in our lives.

Take Heart | It is not easy learning to live with chronic illness, but the patients I counsel are living proof that it is possible. With time one can cultivate the art of acceptance, learning to let some things remain beyond our control. And you don't have to go it alone.

At times, I attend support groups for those living with chronic illness. I always leave these meetings struck by the courage and determination of those attending. They gather as a beacon of hope, a light to shine against darkness. They gain strength from each other, and they affirm that even though they have this condition, the condition does not "have" them. May you, too, arrive at this point in your journey with chronic illness.

CHAPTER II

How to Talk With Your Healthcare Provider

∿

By Karen J. Zielinski, O.S.F.

My friend Janice was shocked with her Stage 3 colorectal cancer diagnosis, since she had just had a colonoscopy two and a half months earlier. She immediately went through a radical resectioning surgery, chemotherapy, and radiation treatments.

She was pleased with her surgeon, nurses, and therapists who were recommended by her doctor's practice. But, it was her oncologist, the "team leader," who called all the shots. She reflected: "I never felt he treated me as an integral part of my health regime. His comments such as, '90% of patients react like this,' made me feel like I was a statistic, not a person."

When Janice had a serious allergic reaction near the end of her chemo, her oncologist recommended that she get a second opinion. Janice jumped at the suggestion; she wanted a healthcare professional who would partner with her.

The new oncologist listened to Janice and he was able to verbalize her concerns even when she could not. He answered all the questions she had written out and said, "Our goal is to eliminate this cancer, to give you back your life." Janice felt comforted. She felt she could now talk comfortably to her health team.

Working your way through | Most of us probably have a healthy, respectful relationship with our healthcare providers. But we might have experienced situations where our doctors have been short with us, kept us waiting, or made us feel they were not "on our side." Despite how vulnerable we feel when we're sick, a doctor who treats us respectfully and compassionately can help us recover faster since our stress level is reduced and our immune system is less taxed. After all, we all deserve respect regardless of our educational backgrounds, occupations, or financial assets. Patients are not less important than their healthcare providers.

Having competent professionals who know how to diagnose and treat us is important, but is only one part of good healthcare. We need a good doctor-patient relationship, one of mutual respect. We owe respect to our doctors and nurses, with their expertise and busy schedules; but they need to respect us, too. We, too, work, raise families, and have busy schedules. When we honestly feel that our doctor is not treating us with courtesy and respect, we owe it to ourselves and our health to let them know how we feel. It might be hard to do, but it is our right to be treated with dignity.

Remember: doctors are not omniscient. Although they have great medical expertise, we actually know our condition best. It is our responsibility to tell them accurately and honestly what we are experiencing physically. Doctors are also not omnipotent—our doctor is not the only one who can help us heal. When our doctor treats us like an active participant, we become partners in our own healing.

✎ *Take responsibility.* Many doctors and healthcare providers perceive they have three separate roles with their patients: to be an educator and

> "Make friends with the doctor, for he is essential to you. God has also established him in his profession."
> —Sirach 38:1

information source, a healthcare manager, and a compassionate listener. If your counselor, physical therapist, nurse, doctor, or technician does not meet all three of these roles, you can do something to improve your situation.

"Tell me and I forget. Teach me and I remember. Involve me and I learn."
—Mark Twain

We are ultimately in charge of our healthcare. When first diagnosed, we might be overwhelmed and unsure of our healthcare decisions. We need someone who communicates with us. Your healthcare provider must be willing to work with you. If you do not feel comfortable, make a change right away. Do not hesitate to get a second opinion. It is overwhelming enough going through a health crisis, and we do not need to add angst and uneasy feelings at this challenging time of treatment.

Sometimes asking family or friends for recommendations can help us find new providers. Finding new health professionals might depend on whether they have offices in your area, or if they are included in your healthcare plan and accepting new patients.

❧ *Participate actively with your healthcare team.* Your healthcare team can consist of the physician leading your care, called your "Attending Physician." With them can be consulting physicians, residents, primary care physicians, nurse practitioners (NP), physician assistants (PA), nurses caring for you in the hospital and in other areas, respiratory, physical, occupational therapists, technicians, dieticians, pharmacists, social workers and case managers, and chaplains. Regardless of who you are working with, you have the right and the responsibility to fully participate in all decisions related to your medical care.

The more your team knows about you and your needs, the better they can help you with your plan of care to help with your recovery. Sometimes it may seem like a member of your team is too busy to address your concerns. If you do not understand what they tell you, or if they talk too fast, be sure to ask questions. It is their job to help you understand your treatment plan. You need to help them understand what they need to tell you so you know exactly what is happening or going to happen. The more you know, the more helpful you are to your total care team.

∾ *Talk to your healthcare professionals.* Members of your healthcare team focus on different things. Know the names of people who come to talk to you. Write down questions or concerns to raise with them. Be sure to take down their names and discussions you have with them. Have a family member or friend come with you to your appointment to help you remember questions and answers. If you are too sick or not up to talking, have someone speak for you. When your health and your life are on the line, you owe it to yourself to exercise due diligence on your own behalf.

Ask members of your team to explain words or procedures you don't know. And remember, your health team may not know the answers to some questions. If your doctor or nurse says, "I don't know," they may not be avoiding answering you, but may need more information about your condition before they can provide a complete answer. This might take more time, but it is important to take the time needed to get the best answers.

"A doctor who cannot take a good history and a patient who cannot give one are in danger of giving and receiving bad treatment."
—Author Unknown

∾ *Remember that your healthcare providers want you to stay healthy!* Healthcare professionals cannot read minds, but they have heard pretty much everything. Try not to be embarrassed or uncomfortable. Sometimes you might not mention what concerns you, thinking the healthcare professional will "just know." Healthcare professionals depend on you to tell them what is going on. To be an active participant in your treatment decisions, it is up to you to share your concerns.

We need to talk to our healthcare providers in a way that will help them to listen. Some ways you can do this are: be prepared for your appointment, arrive on time with all of the information you think is required; be brief, very specific, and factual as you describe your problem; do some advance research which will help you ask relevant questions; speak up if you feel your concerns have not been adequately addressed; share your feelings—tell the professional that you are nervous, hopeful, etc.

Take Heart | Research shows that patients who take an active role in their health decisions will live healthier lives and be more satisfied with their healthcare and treatment results. It can be comforting and critical to your overall good health when you take control of it as much as you can. By learning about your condition, asking your questions, or voicing your concerns or fears, you can take control of your health. Knowledge is power for you. Professionals are more likely to choose the health options that will meet your needs.

You need to do your part. It can be just what the doctor ordered.

CHAPTER III

Dealing With the Frustration of Waiting During a Serious Illness

༃

By Joel Schorn

Some time ago, both the wife and mother of a friend of mine went through cancer diagnoses, surgeries, and treatments. My friend said he will never forget the moments he learned of their illnesses and the shock they produced. Though the feeling of *this can't be happening* felt as it would never lift, it soon gave way to the grind of many months of tests, consultations with doctors, procedures, recoveries, treatments, and follow-up appointments.

The work of dealing with a serious disease involves many challenges: fear, worry, pain and discomfort, stress, and occasional frustration. One experience, though, is constant in the journey through illness: *waiting*.

Working your way through | Whether you are a patient who has a serious illness or a friend or loved one of someone who has one, you're going to do a lot of waiting: for test results, diagnoses, treatment plans, surgery dates, the treatments themselves, recovery, or even sitting in waiting rooms. You can, however, do some things to make the waiting—and also the whole experience of an illness—a little more tolerable.

❧ *Use the time to take advantage of the information available to you.* After you or a friend or loved one are diagnosed with a serious illness, prepare for an avalanche of information, most of it—despite our digital age—in the form of paper. Materials about the disease, descriptions of medications, instructions, financial statements, appointment records, contact information—all of these and more will pile up very quickly.

And that information is important. The more you know about and understand a disease and its treatment, the less fear you will have about the future…and the better you will be able to plan your life around the illness. Most doctors provide packets of information, and many hospitals have staff members dedicated to patient and loved-one education. Take these resources if they're offered to you—and read them!

Information is also available from a number of health and medical websites. In addition, you'll also find a wonderful source for advice from people who have gone through the particular illness you're dealing with or know someone who has. Helpful as these websites and people may be, however, the most important information you get will come directly from the medical professionals you're working with. They're the only ones who can apply the appropriate medical knowledge to your individual case. Every person is different, so it's crucial that you pay close attention to all the information you are receiving—and make sure your ill loved one or friend does, too. And follow the instructions you get—about medications, self-care, diet, activity levels, and other issues—very carefully.

One easy way to manage this mountain of information is to get a good, old-fashioned

> *"What is important is not what someone is, but what they are waiting for. Not the events of life, but its possibilities."*
> —Dorothee Sölle

three-ring binder with dividers and envelopes. Organize your paperwork by category, like "Hospital," "Oncologist," "Cardiologist," "Finances," "Medications," and so on. That way, you'll not only be able to keep track of everything, but you'll also be able to find information quickly when you need it. If you are more inclined to use your computer, there are several helpful websites that will aid you in organizing your information.

"The Lord is good to those who wait for him, to the soul that seeks him."

—Lamentations 3:25

∾ *Develop your waiting room skills.* Whether as a patient or a loved one or friend of one, you're going to get very familiar with waiting areas. Surgeries, tests, other procedures, and follow-up visits can take lots of time—sometimes hours at a stretch—and frequently go longer than anticipated. So it helps to prepare yourself.

First of all, waiting rooms come in several varieties. Some are large, some small; some noisy, some quiet; some crowded, while others have only a few people in them at any one time. Many medical facilities invest a lot in creating comfortable and soothing waiting places, especially in newer facilities, while others do less.

To be ready for these possibilities, bring things to do: reading, work, a laptop (especially if Wi-Fi is available), music you can listen to with headphones—whatever keeps you occupied. My friend was actually able to get quite a bit of work done waiting for his wife or mother. You'll feel productive, and it will get your mind off the situation a bit. Even if you're the patient, expect to wait; if you're accompanying someone, expect to wait longer, sometimes with little or no company. My friend told me he once spent several hours in a waiting room only to look up from what he was doing and find he was the only person in the place—even the desk staff had left!

It's also good to have a Plan B. If you're anticipating a long appointment and don't want to stay in the waiting room for the duration, you can probably find somewhere to spend part of the time, like a hospital cafeteria or nearby coffee shop or restaurant. If you're at a hospital or other large medical facility, you can usually find a quiet alternative seating area. A chapel may also be available for prayer or as a peaceful place to wait. If necessary, let the people at the desk know

"As for me, I will look to the Lord, I will wait for the God of my salvation; my God will hear me."
—Micah 7:7

you're stepping out; and, if you're waiting for someone, tell them where you're going to be and that you can be reached by mobile phone.

Visits related to diagnosing and treating a serious illness can be stressful as well as physically debilitating; so, if at all possible, a patient should have someone along to give them a ride, navigate through corridors, elevators, and doors, or accompany them on public transportation. A companion can also provide emotional support and help keep track of future appointments, new information, and instructions.

∾ *Practice "holy waiting."* Whatever you're waiting for in connection with an illness, you will face the challenge of what to do during the present time before the next appointment, test result, decision about treatment, or piece of news. One approach is to see your waiting as a kind of "holy waiting" or "vigil," prayerful waiting that includes watchfulness. In the many kinds of waiting serious illness requires, you can spend some of that time being watchful and attentive for the presence of God and the movements of God's Spirit in your life. "Wait for the Lord," the Psalmist prays, "be strong, and let your heart take courage; wait for the Lord!" (Psalm 27:14).

Prayer is a way to do that—be it for patience, healing, acceptance, or strength—as are Scripture and other spiritually inspiring reading. Experiences of nature during an illness can be especially powerful because they help you to see that both health and sickness are parts of creation—that everything begins and ends with a good and loving God.

The Bible has many stories of holy waiting. Mary waited for the birth of Jesus. Simeon and Anna waited in the Temple for the appearance of the Messiah, just as John the Baptist waited in the wilderness for the One who was to come after him. Jesus waited in a garden for his arrest, and his disciples waited in an upper room for the promised coming of his Spirit. Holy waiting means looking ahead to something that is not yet here—to a fullness that will complete the present situation.

Such waiting helps you to see and feel that no matter what you or a loved one is going through with a serious illness, God will be there. That expectation, as St. Paul recognized, points to hope: "Now hope that is seen is not hope. For who hopes for what is seen? But if we hope for what we do not see, we wait for it with patience" (Romans 8:24-25).

Take Heart | With a serious illness, you don't always know what's going to happen, but you do know that whatever happens will involve lots of waiting. In these times of uncertainty and anxiety, you can use your waiting to educate yourself and others about the illness and its treatment, pass the hours productively, and even grow closer to God and those you love.

CHAPTER IV

Healing Your Body, Mind, and Spirit Together

❧

By Robert L. Kinast

My brother Don's future looked bright. At 30, he was an award-winning regional manager for a large electronics company, and he was engaged to be married.

Then he began to notice that his vision would sometimes fog and his feet and hands often felt numb. The family doctor referred him to a neurologist who diagnosed the early stages of multiple sclerosis.

Multiple sclerosis is a disease of the central nervous system that damages the protective covering around nerve fibers. Although located in very tiny sections of the body, its impact is felt by the whole person—body, mind, and spirit.

Don's worsening condition caused him to resign from his career and break off his engagement. Eventually, it disrupted his entire lifestyle. At a deeper level, it changed his self-image and made him question his value as a contributing member of society. These changes affected his relationships with family, friends, and even God. Facing these emotional and spiritual challenges was sometimes more demanding for Don than dealing with the physical effects of MS.

Through physical therapy, Don learned to monitor his diet, walk with canes, and perform daily exercises. Encouraged by these achievements, he moved into an apartment equipped for handicapped people, enrolled in a community college, and became active in a local chapter of the MS Society. He also began reading Scripture every day, weaving his experiences into the passages.

None of this was easy and none of it happened instantaneously, but all of it was connected. Don has been able to face MS because he has used every resource of his body, mind, and spirit together.

| *Working your way through* | A major illness, personal loss, emotional problem, or spiritual crisis might originate in |

one area of your life, but it doesn't remain there. You are a complex individual with many different facets, and the events of your life affect every part of you.

On the one hand, it might seem discouraging to think that physical pain or disease cannot be confined to your body but spreads to your emotions and mental outlook and prayer life. And it might feel more comforting to think that emotional stress or spiritual anxiety could never raise your blood pressure or upset the chemical balance in your body. On the other hand, it's encouraging to know that, because all your various dimensions are interrelated, you can call upon all your resources—body, mind, and spirit—to find healing at times of brokenness.

∿ *See yourself as more than a machine.* Science has made remarkable medical advances by analyzing the body as a machine with interlocking parts. When something goes wrong, we call on medical experts to diagnose the problem and fix it. But you are not a machine and neither is your body.

The trick is to hear the music that is the body. If we can do so, the meaning of the body can be transformed. It becomes not a blind, silent, doomed machine but a glorious composition, a part of God's oeuvre: the Great Tome.

—Larry Dossey,
Meaning and Medicine

In the view of Dr. Larry Dossey, author of *Meaning and Medicine*, your body is more like music than a machine. It is a harmony of movements and patterns that flows in and out of the harmonies emitted by those around you, including plants and animals. This condition of harmony is often called "wellness" or, simply, "health." Health is not static like a machine but is rather a constant and continuous process, like an unfinished symphony, absorbing what is happening so that it can shape the next movement.

> *"True wholeness comes from having a love affair with life, living in harmony with inner wisdom, and coming to a full sense of awe at the miracle of one's own existence."*
>
> —Psychotherapist M. Keith, O.S.F.

My brother's multiple sclerosis severely disrupted the health he had known before. He could have thought of himself simply as broken down or he could have hoped for someone else to fix his problem. Instead, he redefined what wellness could mean for him; he created a new harmony, using all of his resources. Many other courageous individuals have struggled to find such a new harmony when their spouse or child died, when a loved one became addicted, when their lifestyle was drastically altered due to some unchangeable circumstance.

༄ *Get your problem into perspective.* A serious illness or emotional problem or spiritual dilemma tends to dominate your awareness. Often people even identify themselves or others in terms of their condition: "a heart patient," "a diabetic," "a widow," "a recovering alcoholic."

For a while my brother thought of himself only as an MS victim and was aware only of what he could no longer do. After he moved into his own apartment, began attending college courses, and met new people, he gradually became able to think of himself as Don, who also has MS. He went from being overwhelmed by his illness to putting it in its place within the entire perspective of his life.

The ability to deal with a crisis by putting it within the context of your whole life is

People today, in order to restore themselves to a whole, require a holistic approach to living. This entails being a faithful servant to one's self—a focus on the mind, body, and spirit. A holistic lifestyle... emphasizes freedom to explore and discover God in recreation, nature, and people.
—Psychotherapist M. Keith, O.S.F.

part of *holistic* healing. The problem takes its proper place in the framework of your entire life, with no greater and no less importance than it realistically deserves. Often when people go through a divorce, for example, they initially think of themselves as a complete failure. They can experience healing if they are able to put this one experience into the context of all their efforts and achievements, in the marriage as well as in other areas of life.

❧ *Develop an image of your life.* One of the first steps toward holistic healing is simply to depict your life through some kind of an image. An image captures your feelings as a whole, all at once. It gives you a picture of yourself and your situation. How does it feel to be the person you are now, including the illness or problem that is now part of your life?

People with serious illnesses frequently use military images to describe their experience. The disease invades the body; they put up a strong defense; they hope to conquer it. Alcoholics may refer to their "marriage" to the bottle and addicts may talk about being "imprisoned" by the needle. Develop your own personalized image that captures for you the experience of your life at this point in time.

Reframe your image. The image which emerges from a situation of stress or pain is usually not very appealing. It describes how you actually feel, not how you would like to feel. To move toward healing, you need to reframe your image, to look at it from a different angle.

Other people can be very helpful at this point, offering insights that might not occur to you and enabling you to reframe your experience. Though nothing in your actual situation may change, you may find yourself able to look at it in a different light. Instead of seeing it as a liability, you can begin to see it as an opportunity for more meaningful living.

Prayer is a powerful resource for reframing your situation. Prayer enlarges your perspective by enabling you to open yourself to God's influence, so that God's encompassing vision can enter. In prayer you let God stimulate and shape your imagination so you can look at yourself from God's point of view. A woman who struggled with bouts of depression, for example, reframed her experience when she meditated on her down moods as a "gift of tears."

Similarly, a group of elderly residents in a retirement home reframed their image in light of a story in the Gospel of John (5:1-9). In that story a sick man had been waiting for someone to carry him to the pool and its healing waters. Jesus told him simply to stand up and walk. Applying this story to themselves, the residents began to initiate activities on their own and live a more complete, meaningful life together.

When an image is reframed in an appealing way, it prompts you to act on it. In addition, prayer and meditation stimulate your confidence and ability to act. As you do, you begin to experience greater well-being and wholeness.

Take Heart | There is no cure for multiple sclerosis—just as there is no cure for the death of a loved one, the loss of a one-time opportunity, the trauma of a severe disappointment. But there is more to you and your life than what you are now suffering. If you can harmonize the power of your body, mind, and spirit, you will set in motion a creative process that will nurture the healing of your whole self.

CHAPTER V

Spiritual Practices for Coping With Serious Illness

❧

By Mary Kendrick Moore

Years ago, after a serious hospitalization and months of recovery, I sat on the beach one gloomy day. I felt the power of the waves rolling onto the shore. They became a metaphor for this interruption that had washed over my life. I walked down the shore, took out my journal, and wrote: *Out there the tiny white caps wave as if they want to speak. The ripples move in until they finally begin to swell. And then the wave rolls all over itself crashing into the shore cresting with the force behind it.*

While I walked amid the beauty of nature and recorded my deep feelings, my grief over the changes in my life and my body found a voice. The spiritual practice of journaling nurtured my faith and strengthened my inner spirit, and opened a path for me through the dark days of uncertainty.

Working your way through | Illness can feel like a force that will consume you, just as ocean waves seem to swallow up all that is in their path. Yet with any serious diagnosis, you can traverse these waves in a way that can bring hope and healing. As you journey through your emotions and face challenging decisions, the 10 spiritual practices that follow offer suggestions for you to explore.

❧ *Learning.* During illness it's easy to become overwhelmed and isolated. Though much more intense, coping with illness is like any project or process that you have never done or have put aside for a long time. Certain skills and pointers help. Talk to people, perhaps in a support group, who are facing similar circumstances, and learn about their experiences. Seek answers for your questions through your healthcare team, library books, articles, or online newsletters.

Ask your pastor or faith leader to introduce you to someone who has coped with a similar experience, and explore with them how faith is a part of this journey. Open your mind to others by exploring the wisdom of great spiritual writers.

❧ *Writing*. Putting your thoughts, questions, and feelings on paper is a powerful means of self-expression that may help you combat any urge to keep your fear, anxiety, or sadness bottled up inside. Write letters or emails to a few close friends, particularly ones who have experienced a serious illness themselves. Writing poetry or prose often pulls words from the depth of your soul, voicing inner confusion and promoting healing. Keep a journal of your experiences and questions, remembering to include your feelings toward God and your questions about faith.

❧ *Giving*. Serious illness can leave you feeling imprisoned by unexpected circumstances that may confine you to your home or the hospital. Almost without fail, people I encounter who cope well with illness say, "I will not be held captive by this disease." Break the bond by giving of yourself to others, even when you are down.

Benedictine Sister Joan Chittister calls hospitality "the

The caged bird sings with a fearful trill of things unknown but longed for still and his tune is heard on the distant hill for the caged bird sings of freedom.
—Maya Angelou

unboundaried heart." Your choices will depend on the severity of your illness. Maybe you can volunteer to lead a support group in your church or synagogue, address envelopes for your faith community, or mail a simple card to a friend.

> *"God is our refuge and our strength, a very present help in trouble."*
>
> —Psalm 46:1-2

Make a donation to your favorite charity as a way of finding meaning. Giving shifts your focus from your own pain, even if momentarily, and is a means of continuing to embrace the call of God to love others.

↬ *Praying.* The psalmist in Hebrew scripture captures the essence of coping with difficult circumstances: "I sink in deep mire, where there is no foothold; I have come into deep waters, and the flood sweeps over me. I am weary with my crying; my throat is parched. My eyes grow dim with waiting for my God" (Psalm 69:2-3). With that passage as your example, you are invited to bring your honest troubles and emotions before God. Try reading a psalm, and then write it in your own words, making it your own prayer.

Create a small sacred space in your house, with candles and symbols of your faith. Place your hands in a bowl of water to remind you of God's creation. Call to mind one thing you can be grateful for.

∿ *Retreating.* When times are tough, there is nothing like getting away—a vacation, a night out—to retreat from your stress. Planning a retreat while ill requires more preparation, but it's not impossible. Consider a weekend at a spiritual retreat center, and, if needed, ask a friend to drive. Arrange a family trip to a favorite location, but talk with your healthcare team first.

When travel is not possible, find ways to retreat in place: sit on a bench beside a stream, turn your rocking chair toward the sunset, or let your mind roam to different worlds at a local museum or in a book or on a website filled with photography, art, or nature scenes.

∿ *Worshiping.* Rely on faith and on worship traditions that are meaningful to you. When we worship, we seek to bring our needs and hurts before God and to acknowledge and honor God's presence.

Ring the bells that still can ring,
Forget your perfect offering.
There is a crack in everything.
That's how the light gets in.
—Leonard Cohen,
Stranger Music

Worship embraces the fact that we are part of a larger community, something that is especially important during illness. Let worship be a time when you say things to God and to others, such as *I am hurting, I need your support, I want you to walk with me.*

✎ *Meditating.* Through quiet reflection, guided imagery, or silent awareness, meditation is often practiced as a means of relieving stress and pain. This quieting of your soul offers a spiritual sanctuary from the complexities of illness.

Begin learning this practice by simply breathing deeply, taking slow breaths in and out for several minutes. Then try adding a phrase from a song or scripture as you take your breaths. Explore deeper practices of meditation with a teacher or class.

✎ *Moving.* After a serious car accident in which I suffered seven broken ribs, I despaired over my inability to get around as I had been accustomed to. I couldn't pick up my toddler daughter and could hardly even stand.

Depression can brew quickly under these circumstances, and it's important to engage your inner strength to keep moving as your condition permits. After you stand up once, set a goal to take three steps. After you walk 100 feet, walk 200 feet the next time. When walking is not possible, stretch your ankles or exercise your arms. Try a yoga class. With the consultation of your healthcare professionals, find the best activities for you that will balance both pacing and pushing yourself.

❧ *Looking and listening.* Open your heart and mind each day to something outside of yourself and your suffering. Listen for the encouraging voice of a friend. Look for the signs of our amazing God-given ability to rise above life's most difficult experiences.

Open a window to feel the wind. Ask a friend to put a birdhouse outside your window. Walk outside and feel the rain. Smell the scent of a candle or a new bar of lavender soap. Listen to a child read you a story. Be alert for the voice of God that comes through ordinary moments in your day.

❧ *Singing.* Poet Maya Angelou proclaimed in one of her poems, "I know why a caged bird sings." She writes that even when "his wings are clipped and his feet are tied," he opens his throat to sing.

There is nothing like illness to leave us feeling as if our wings are clipped. But we have a choice either to close ourselves off in the darkness of fear and anger or to seek the light of our spirits which the darkness can't squelch. Sing. Even if you don't sing, sing. Hum a tune that has touched you. Ask someone else to sing. Play music—from gentle soothing hymns to rousing pop music to Latin salsa. Something changes within you when you sing; your spirit starts to look for its dancing shoes.

Take Heart | At the end of my ocean visit, the sun peeked through the gray clouds and I wrote these words: *White foam ripples into the curve of the shoreline and the power subsides leaving a sheet of glass to reflect the light of the sun.*

In all faith traditions, God is the author of compassion and engages in the spirit of healing. Facing our illness and allowing the waves of sadness and stress to rush over us opens the door for healing. Practice spiritual disciplines that make hope possible, and you will find the strength and light within you that calms your spirit and heals your soul.

About the Authors

Rev. Daniel H. Grossoehme, B.C.C., *is chaplain for the Division of Pulmonary Medicine at Cincinnati Children's Hospital Medical Center, and assistant professor in the University of Cincinnati Department of Pediatrics.*

Karen J. Zielinski, O.S.F., *was Director of Communications for the Sisters of St. Francis of Sylvania, Ohio, from 1991 to 2008. Currently serving as Director of Canticle Studio, a creative office of products which focus on spirituality and health, she is a regular contributor to local and national health publications and other journals. Her first book,* Hope and Help for Living with Illness *(Franciscan Media) deals with health and spirituality. Sister Karen has lived with multiple sclerosis since 1975.*

Joel Schorn *is an editor and writer living in Chicago. He is the author of a number of* CareNotes *and* PrayerNotes *as well as* Holy Simplicity: Mother Teresa, Dorothy Day, and Thérèse of Lisieux *and* God's Doorkeepers: Padre Pio, Solanus Casey, and André Bessette, *both from Servant Books.*

Robert L. Kinast *is a priest of the Archdiocese of Atlanta. He has taught pastoral theology since 1977 and is currently the director of the Center for Theological Reflection at Madeira Beach, Florida. His latest book, published by Eerdmans, is a study of St. John's Gospel entitled* If Only You Recognized God's Gift.

Rev. Mary Kendrick Moore, B.C.C., *is a minister in the United Church of Christ, a pastor, healthcare chaplain, and freelance writer.*